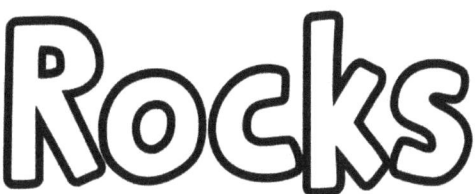

DISCOVER PICTURES AND FACTS ABOUT ROCKS FOR KIDS!

No part of this book may be reproduced or used in any way or form or by any means whether electronic or mechanical, this means that you cannot record or photocopy any material ideas or tips that are provided in this book.

Copyright 2020

Rocks are cool, and they can be fun to collect. Here are 10 facts about rocks that rock!

They are naturally formed, and they're made up of minerals

The surface we stand on, the crust of the earth is made up of rock

These have been used by humans as early tools, weapons, and even construction materials, and is one of the earliest forms of tools

You have three different rock types, and they are igneous, metamorphic, and sedimentary, which are distinguished by how they're formed

Rocks actually go through a cycle, where they change from each rock type over time

Metamorphic rocks are created with heat and pressure, and they're found within the earth where there's enough pressure for it to form

Igneous rocks are made when volcanoes erupt, and this is the hot, molten rock that forms

Sedimentary rocks are made with sediment compacted together, so the rocks within bodies of water are these types

There are even rocks in space, but those are called meteorites, and they have different elements

Ores are actually a type of rock that has minerals and other important parts in it, such as gold and silver

Rocks are cool, and you learned some cool facts about rocks and why they matter

Ingram Content Group UK Ltd.
Milton Keynes UK
UKHW052128250723
425779UK00006B/55